EMANUEL SWEDENBORG (1688-1772) is acknowledged as one of the great thinkers of the eighteenth century and a pioneering figure in the history of Western thought. Philosopher, theologian, visionary, scientist and statesman, his book *Heaven and Hell* has had a direct influence on William Blake, Honoré de Balzac, Gerard de Nerval, W B Yeats, S T Coleridge, Fyodor Dostoevsky and many others, and his theory of correspondences is rightly understood as one of the defining influences on Romantic and Symbolist thought. More recently, through the work of Czesław Miłosz, Italo Calvino, A S Byatt and Iain Sinclair, we see his name re-emerge in relation to 'pyschogeography', 'historical realism' and 'magical realism'. Jorge Luis Borges once described him as the most extraordinary man in recorded history. *Introducing Swedenborg: Correspondences* is the second in a series of pocket introductions providing accessible essays on his thought and influence.

GARY LACHMAN was a founding member of the seminal rock group Blondie with whom he was inducted into the Rock and Roll Hall of Fame in 2006. He is the author of many books on a range of esoteric, literary and countercultural themes. For the Swedenborg Society he has written *Into the Interior: Discovering Swedenborg* (2009) which was republished by Tarcher as *Swedenborg: an Introduction to his Life and Ideas* (2012).

TITLES IN THE SERIES

1. *Introducing Swedenborg*
PETER ACKROYD

2. *Introducing Swedenborg: Correspondences*
GARY LACHMAN

Introducing Swedenborg:

Correspondences

Introducing Swedenborg:
Correspondences

GARY LACHMAN

The Swedenborg Society
20-21 Bloomsbury Way
London
WC1A 2TH

2021

Typeset at Swedenborg House
Printed at TJ Books Limited, Padstow
Introducing Swedenborg: Correspondences

Series editor: Stephen McNeilly

Copy editors: Avery Curran and James Wilson

Published by:
The Swedenborg Society
Swedenborg House
20-21 Bloomsbury Way
London WC1A 2TH

ISBN: 978-085448-216-0
British Library Cataloguing-in-Publication Data.
A catalogue record for this book
is available from the British Library.

Contents

Chronology

1688 Born Emanuel Swedberg on 29 January.

1709 He graduates from Uppsala University and publishes his first work, *Selected Sentences.*

1710 He travels to London and attends lectures by Isaac Newton and studies with Edmond Halley and John Flamsteed. George Berkeley publishes *A Treatise Concerning the Principles of Human Knowledge.*

1714-15 He drafts designs for a series of novel inventions, including a water clock, a submarine and an airplane. King Louis XIV of France dies and is succeeded by his grandson, Louis XV, aged 5. Emanuel publishes three volumes of poetry. G W Leibniz writes *Monadology*.

1716-18 Emanuel is introduced to King Charles XII of Sweden and he publishes Sweden's first scientific journal.

1718 He declines an invitation to become Professor of Astronomy at Uppsala University, Sweden.

1719 The Swedberg family is ennobled and Emanuel's name is changed to Swedenborg. He takes a seat in the Swedish House of Nobles.

1723 Swedenborg's appointment to the role of extraordinary assessor on the Swedish Board of Mines is confirmed.

1724 Swedenborg declines an invitation to succeed Nils Celsius as Professor of Astronomy at Uppsala University.

1726 *Gulliver's Travels* by Jonathan Swift is published.

1727 J S Bach composes *St Matthew Passion.* Isaac Newton dies.

1734 Swedenborg publishes his philosophical and scientific *magnum opus*, *Opera Philosophica et Mineralia* in Leipzig where J S Bach is Musical Director at St Thomas Church. Swedenborg is invited to correspond with the Russian Academy of Sciences.

1736-8 He travels to Paris and Venice to study anatomy and drafts a study of the brain resulting in two large unpublished manuscripts entitled *The Cerebrum* and *The Brain*.

1740-1 He is nominated into the Swedish Academy of Sciences by his cousin Carl Linneaus and publishes *The Economy of the Animal Kingdom* with Voltaire's printer and bookseller François Changuion. This work introduces his science of correspondences.

1743 Swedenborg buys a house and plot of land in Hornsgatan, Stockholm. This is the year in which he is first addressed by a spirit.

1743-4 In a private journal, published after his death as the *Journal of Dreams*, Swedenborg describes having a vision of Christ.

1744-5 Swedenborg publishes his *The Animal Kingdom* and *The Worship and Love of God*, and begins a multi-volume study of the Old Testament entitled *The Word Explained*.

1747 He resigns from the Board of Mines. He also begins his *Spiritual Diary* which he continues for nearly 20 years but leaves unpublished.

1748 David Hume publishes *An Enquiry Concerning Human Understanding*.

1749-56 Swedenborg publishes his most important work, an eight-volume biblical exegesis *Arcana Caelestia* which is printed anonymously in London by John Lewis and John Hart.

1753 Carl Linnaeus publishes *Species Plantarum*.

1755 The Lisbon earthquake.

1757 Swedenborg writes of a 'Last Judgment' in the spirit world. William Blake is born.

1758 Whilst in London, Swedenborg publishes 5 works printed as supplements to his *Arcana Caelestia*. These are: *The Worlds in Space*, *The Last Judgment*, *The New Jerusalem*, *The White Horse* and his most famous and widely read work *Heaven and Hell*.

1757-9 During this time he also begins a multi-volume commentary on the Book of Revelation entitled *The Apocalypse Explained*. He prepares it for the press but decides, for reasons still unknown, not to publish.

1759 Voltaire publishes *Candide.*

1762 Jean-Jacques Rousseau publishes *Emile, or On Education.* Immanuel Kant writes to Swedenborg. Swedenborg indicates he will offer a reply in a forthcoming work.

1763 In Amsterdam Swedenborg publishes 4 new works on the theme of the New Jerusalem and a small work on the Last Judgment. *Divine Love and Wisdom* is published soon after and is thought to be his response to Kant.

1764 Swedenborg publishes *Divine Providence*.

1766 Immanuel Kant publishes his book on Swedenborg later translated into English as *Dreams of a Spirit Seer*. That year Swedenborg publishes *The Apocalypse Revealed*.

1767 Premier of Wolfgang Amadeus Mozart's first

opera *Apollo et Hyacinthus*, in Salzburg.

1768 Swedenborg publishes *Conjugial Love* and for the first time puts his name on the title page of his theological works.

1769 In London and Amsterdam he publishes *The Interaction of the Soul & Body* and *Brief Exposition of the Doctrines of the New Church.* A controversy breaks out in Sweden regarding the publication of *Conjugial Love* and his books are confiscated.

1771 Swedenborg travels to Amsterdam and publishes *The True Christian Religion* then travels to London. When in London he suffers from a stroke but partially recovers.

1772 He writes to John Wesley and on Sunday 29 March, Swedenborg dies.

Without a good knowledge of correspondences, no one can have a clear picture of anything about the spiritual world, of its flowing into the natural world, and nor of the spiritual in relation to the natural. Also, not a thing can be known of the human spirit called the soul, and its operation on the body; nor of the human condition after death. For all these reasons therefore it is necessary to say what correspondence is, and what its nature is. In this way a path will be prepared for what is to follow.

—Swedenborg, *Heaven and Hell*, §88

One of the most important ideas—and arguably the most influential—that has come down to us from the work of the eighteenth-century Swedish savant Emanuel Swedenborg is his doctrine of correspondences. In the years that followed Swedenborg's proclaiming this doctrine, in works like the eight-volume *Arcana Coelestia*,[1] his 'inner' reading of Genesis and Exodus—although proclaiming is hardly the word for Swedenborg's sedate Latin prose—its influence ranged far and wide, not only in the religious, spiritual and philosophical spheres in which we might have expected it to have an impact, but also in artistic, cultural and even political ones. Less than twenty years after Swedenborg's death in 1772, his ideas about the links between heaven and earth informed elements of the French Revolution, his notion of the 'regenerated man' being applied to society at large. And it is no exaggeration to say that the most successful adaptation of Swedenborg's doctrine of correspondences appeared in the artistic, literary and musical developments associated with the Symbolist movement of the late nineteenth century. This produced poets like Arthur Rimbaud, painters like Gustave Moreau, and composers like Claude Debussy, among many others, and in many ways remains with us today.

Although Symbolism was based on a misunderstanding of Swedenborg's idea, or at least a modification of it by the nineteenth-century French poet Charles Baudelaire—which we will look at further on—it is no small feat for an insight previously occupying the fringe of consciousness to have such an effect on the wider public. Yet its influence did not end there, and in more recent times, Swedenborg's correspondences have reappeared in places that, I suspect, may have surprised him.

For example, the 'law of attraction' which informs many of today's bestselling self-help, New Thought, 'positive thinking' and 'prosperity gospel' philosophies, by which one's thoughts can help one to 'grow rich', is based on another misunderstanding of Swedenborg's ideas. Swedenborg's 'law of attraction' is not about drawing prosperity to oneself; it is the pull one feels toward either heaven or hell, following a requisite stay in the spirit world after bodily death. Depending on our 'true affections'—what we really love—we gravitate to either one or the other, an idea later embraced by the nineteenth-century American spiritualist Andrew Jackson Davis. And this in essence is the result of Swedenborg's insight that the kind of world we inhabit—either here or in the afterlife—depends on the kinds of thoughts we entertain; the one corresponds to the other. As Swedenborg said, heaven and hell are inside us. But the only riches Swedenborg associated with this arrangement were spiritual, not material ones.

What did Swedenborg mean by correspondences? Simply put, the doctrine of correspondences states that everything in the natural world—minerals, plants, animals, stars, planets—is related in a specific way to the higher, spiritual worlds. As Swedenborg writes, 'The whole of the natural world corresponds to (or has a counterpart in) the spiritual world, not only in general, but also in single details'.[2] Everything we see around us is a reflection of the worlds above. As the German poet Goethe, a great reader of Swedenborg, and like him a scientist, put it in his drama *Faust*, 'Alles Vergängliche/ Ist nur ein Gleichnis',[3] all that is transitory is but a symbol. That is, it is a sign for something else. For Swedenborg, that something else is the spiritual world.

As Swedenborg sees it, this relationship is rather like that of a word to its meaning, or of the human face to the thoughts and feelings it expresses, with the one 'standing for', or corresponding to, the other. We can write down a word, type it out on our computer screens, or say it, but its meaning is something more than our pixels, script or sound, something more, that is, than its physical carrier. The meaning of a word is an 'inner' experience, something we grasp with our mind in the same way that Swedenborg grasped the inner meaning of the Bible. And for Swedenborg this is true of the spiritual world as well.

For Swedenborg then, what we experience here in the natural world is, we might say, like a kind of alphabet, or perhaps a book, in which the spiritual world communicates to us. As the Nobel Prize-winning writer Czesław Miłosz put it, 'Swedenborg's world is all language'.[4] A tree, a flower, a cloud, are not only physical phenomena, but words, embodied meanings, which we may not know how to decipher, but which remain meaningful nonetheless, rather like difficult mathematical formulae which, abstruse to us, convey pertinent information to those in the know. It may be that for the time being, we can perceive only the physical aspect of phenomena. But it may come to pass that, as Swedenborg did, we will at some point see their inner meaning too. Then we will learn how to perform, as one of Swedenborg's keenest interpreters, the Iranologist Henry Corbin, describes it, a 'spiritual hermeneutics',[5] not on this or that sacred book, but on the text of the world itself.

*

This correspondence between the natural and the spiritual worlds is true, Swedenborg tells us, of man-made things too. The buildings we live in, the streets we walk, the clothes we wear, and the company we keep, these too have spiritual counterparts. In fact, for Swedenborg, this everyday world of space, time and matter that we know so well and which modern science has explored down to its elementary particles, is rooted in the spiritual world, and would not last a second, if the correspondence between the two were broken, rather as an image in a mirror would vanish if its original suddenly disappeared. 'It must be recognized', he tells us, 'that the natural world comes into existence and maintains that existence from the spiritual world, just like an effect from the cause that brings it about'.[6] And just as there is something of the creator in each of his creations, so too there is something in our world of the worlds that bring it into being. They correspond with ours.

In Swedenborg's vision of reality, our earthly, physical, material world—the one we perceive and enjoy through our senses—is on the lowest rung of a kind of ladder of worlds, with higher ones reaching above us, into realms beyond the physical, an arrangement not unfamiliar in the Western esoteric tradition, within which Swedenborg occupies an important place. These higher worlds, with the Divine at the top and successive stages below, participate in ours, and are not entirely unlike our own. Much of what we find here, we can find there too, albeit in a form rather different from what we are familiar with here on earth. Things we find here correspond, Swedenborg tells us, to things we will find there, and one of his aims in developing his doctrine of correspondences was to educate his readers in how to understand the language in which the higher speaks to the lower.

We may not be able to understand this language immediately, but to say it speaks in a foreign tongue is not quite correct, nor is it true to say that the key to it is entirely lost. The language of correspondences, Swedenborg tells us, is not lost, only forgotten. We possessed it once long ago, in what Swedenborg and many others see as a Golden Age. 'Correspondence?' he asks. 'People today do not really know what that is'. But it 'was different with people who lived in the very earliest times'. To them 'the knowledge of correspondences was pre-eminent among all the branches of knowledge'.[7] This may not be the case now—indeed for us, as for Gertrude Stein, a rose is a rose and little else, perhaps even less.[8] But with work, determination, luck—and not a little grace—we may be able to make it so again.

*

Most readers familiar with Swedenborg's ideas about correspondences first discovered them in the accounts he gave of his journeys to heaven, hell and the spirit world—an intermediary, Purgatory-like realm—in *Arcana Caelestia*, and which he collected in *Heaven and Hell*, certainly his most popular work. There readers discover higher spiritual worlds that are in many ways like this one, but in many other ways, radically different. What first strikes readers of these otherworldly vignettes is the quaint, often homely descriptions Swedenborg gives of life among the angels. In heaven angels live in houses, have jobs, are married, eat, drink and make love—quite often in fact, if Swedenborg's book, *Conjugial Love*,[9] written in his eighties, is any gauge. Swedenborg portrays the domestic and civic affairs of his angels with copious matter-of-fact detail, setting his report on the afterlife very much apart from that of most theologians. They, as Swedenborg's forthright follower William Blake commented, usually refer to an 'allegorical abode to which existence hath never come'.[10] If this is true, it is clear they did not visit Swedenborg's heaven.

Indeed, Swedenborg's robust and concrete higher worlds are rather like similar reports obtained by some members of the Society for Psychical Research in the early part of the last century. For instance, the physicist and paranormal investigator Sir Oliver Lodge published a book in 1916, *Raymond or Life and Death*, about his dead son. In it, 'Raymond'—or a spirit purporting to be him—told his father about conditions in the other world. There people wore robes, ate, smoked cigars and enjoyed the occasional whisky and soda.[11] In 1928, Revd Charles Drayton Thomas published *Life Beyond Death With Evidence*, an account of the other side provided by his deceased father and sister, courtesy of a psychic 'medium'. Here, the spirits speak of roads which are 'unlike the stone or macadamised roads of England' and of a London that enjoys some 'likeness in the parks and beautiful buildings' of earthly London, but which is 'much finer'. In this spiritual London there are horses, dogs and cats, but 'no snakes or lions' and, regrettably, 'very few monkeys'.[12] Other reports present similar accounts of what the philosopher Nietzsche might have called an 'all too human' heaven.[13]

This kind of 'it's just like earth, but only better' vision of the higher realms turned some people away from Swedenborg, and not only theologians. For these folk, stories of angelic communities, dinners, daily chores and other heavenly parallels with 'the trivial round, the common task'—which, according to the hymn, 'should furnish all we ask'[14]—were a bit much to swallow. This may be understandable, although a heaven in which spirits can still drink spirits should not be sneezed at. But Swedenborg's depiction of a kind of embodied afterlife is part of his fundamental vision of reality. In this, the Divine, who radiates through all the worlds, enjoys in essence a human form. Indeed, for Swedenborg, the Divine must take on some visible form; if not, we would not be able to grasp the meaning of creation. We can, as Goethe did, consider the natural world the 'living garment of God', [15] the clothing the Divine wears in deference to we humans, the face it turns towards us and whose expression we read. This of course does not mean that reality has eyes, a nose and a mouth, or not literally at least. What it means is that what we find in ourselves we will find in the other worlds too. In fact, we are our own access to them.

This is because of what Swedenborg calls the *Maximus Homo* or Grand (or Great) Man. I should point out that Swedenborg does not mean 'male' over 'female'; *homo* in Latin includes both sexes in the idea of the human. For Swedenborg,

God, the holy and sacred, is not, as the theologian Rudolf Otto argued, 'wholly other', [16] meaning of some character essentially non-human. This is how the tradition of negative theology, which alludes to God and the Divine by differentiating it from any predicate or limitation, has it. Nor does Swedenborg mean to reduce the spiritual to the 'only human', or to raise the 'all too human' into some kind of deity. That transformation, we could say, is what the modern world has accomplished. What he means is that we are made, as the Bible tells us, in God's image.

Again, this does not mean that we have long white beards and wear robes, but that what we find in our human selves is a reflection of what we find in the Divine. We correspond to it. And what one finds as Swedenborg takes us on a tour of heaven—or to its dark antipode, hell—is that although in appearance they seem rather like home, the fabric of their reality is actually quite different. There, time, space and all the other fundamental means through which we experience existence are altogether other. As I explain in my book about Swedenborg, what we experience here as different points in time and different places in space are, in the spiritual world, experienced as different levels of consciousness, different inner states. The spiritual sun's course through the heavenly year is not marked by days and months, but by changes of consciousness, and intensities of inner states.[17]

*

Swedenborg tells us that he developed his doctrine of correspondences in order to perceive and proclaim the inner meaning of the Bible, what we can call its esoteric reading. He believed that the Bible should not be read as a literal, factual account of creation and all that followed, which is how many fundamentalist Christians do read it—and how fundamentalists of other religions read their own holy scriptures. The Bible should be read instead as a kind of code, using the language of mundane things to symbolize or 'stand for' spiritual things. Just as there are different levels of reality, which Swedenborg refers to as the celestial, spiritual and natural worlds, each one a bit further away from the Divine, so too are there different levels of meaning in Scripture. Swedenborg intended to submit the entire Bible to his close esoteric reading, but after devoting eight volumes to just Genesis and Exodus, he stopped, understandably perhaps. The only other book that he devoted equal attention to was the Book of Revelation. This was enough to begin the new exegesis that would inform the new age, which Swedenborg believed began in 1757.

The idea of reading the Bible symbolically or anagogically—meaning related to spiritual rather than natural reality—was not radically new. One of the early Church Fathers, Clement of Alexandria, adopted the practice of reading Scripture symbolically, rather than as a text to be taken literally. We can grasp the difference between these two ways of understanding through a look at the role metaphor plays in our everyday speech. If someone says 'water under the bridge', we know that this means some event in the past that no longer affects the present; it or we have moved on. Yet at some point, someone first made the connection just as someone at some point first characterized a thorough search as 'leaving no stone unturned'. We use these phrases unthinkingly, which means that they have passed from being 'live' fresh metaphors to being clichés. But as the historian and philosopher of language Owen Barfield tells us, paying attention to the metaphors we take for granted can have a peculiar effect; it can trigger a flash of insight into how pictorial and figurative our language is.[18]

This is another way of seeing language as symbolic, that is as a means of establishing a 'correspondence' between things. Someone of a literal turn of mind—itself a metaphor (in what direction does a mind 'turn'?)—would ask what bridge you were talking about and which stones. This suggests that in an intuitive, practical way, we are already familiar with correspondences, with the idea or practice, that is, of having something 'stand for' something else.

What Clement of Alexandria did—and Origen, another early Church Father who followed him—was to apply this insight to reading Scripture. It was necessary to understand the different levels of meaning to Scripture because not everyone could read it in the same way. This was because different people are at different stages of spiritual development and understanding. And the three-tiered understanding of Scripture that Clement and Origen developed originated in an idea of reality that we can call 'emanationist'. This is a view, shared by many different traditions, that reality is structured hierarchically, with God or the One or some other non-manifest source at the start, out of which 'emanates' the different levels of being in descending order, rather as light from a lamp lessens in brightness the further it moves from the bulb. The idea is generally associated with Neoplatonism—a product, with Clement and Origen, of ancient Alexandria— but it can be found in other traditions, such as cabbala. Swedenborg was familiar with and studied both of them.

In Swedenborg's system, the descending order was different from how Clement and Origen saw things, but their view was close enough to his for our purposes. Clement was eager to establish a higher reading of Scripture—meaning a symbolic one—because the Gnostics, early rivals of the church, were drawing the faithful away by their more sophisticated interpretation of the gospels. He borrowed from the Gnostics the idea of levels of understanding, which he called the 'heathen', the 'believer', and the 'gnostic', meaning one who 'knows'.[19] A heathen reading is a literal one, the believer grasps that the parables are stories teaching something—he has, we can say, a psychological understanding—but a gnostic is able to grasp the inner, esoteric, spiritual meaning behind the words.

I should point out that it was the Jewish philosopher Philo of Alexandria who may have started the practice in the first place. He argued that the Bible should be read allegorically. Genesis, he said, was a 'metaphor for the history of the soul' [20] and not an account of how the world was made. Philo also introduced the idea of the 'Great Chain of Being', the hierarchical view of reality, shared by Clement, Origen and Swedenborg, into the study of the Bible. And of course the Jewish mystical tradition of cabbala is centred on a spiritual reading of the Old Testament, in which not only the words, but the letters of the Hebrew alphabet have deep esoteric significance as well as magical powers. In more recent times, Maurice Nicoll, a Jungian psychologist who became a student of the Russian philosopher P D Ouspensky, devoted two books, *The New Man* and *The Mark*, [21] to an esoteric reading of the gospels, from the point of view of Ouspensky's philosophy. Nicoll, too, was a great reader of Swedenborg, as his five-volume *Psychological Commentaries On the Teachings of G. I. Gurdjieff and P. D. Ouspensky* and his important book *Living Time and the Integration of the Life* reveal.[22]

This kind of inner reading was not limited to Scripture. Porphyry, a follower of the philosopher Plotinus, and one of the great Neoplatonic thinkers, argued that the Greek myths should be read in this esoteric way. In *The Cave of the Nymphs*[23] he gave us his inner reading of Homer. This notion of reading stories of gods and goddesses, not as literal truths or cautionary tales, but as symbolic accounts of the soul, of inner not outer events, went back to Plotinus' teacher, Ammonius Saccas (175-242), who also introduced the idea of three levels of understanding. He applied this to his students, separating them into novices, initiates and masters. He also seems to have had an outer teaching for the public, which he declared in the market place—or on the docks, where he often taught—and an inner one reserved for his closest disciples.

*

Swedenborg, then, was not alone in wanting to develop a way of reading Scripture that revealed its deeper, inner significance, and not merely its literal meaning, what it said on the surface. For him Scripture should be read as a kind of spiritual guidebook, rather than a cosmological and historical text. Yet Swedenborg's reading was not the same as Clement's or Origen's or, for that matter, any other esoteric reading of the Bible. This is not to say that it differed so much from theirs as to make his, and theirs, arbitrary, strictly 'subjective', like a kind of private language. People like Goethe, Blake, Henry Corbin, whom I've mentioned, and the many others who read Swedenborg with profit that I haven't mentioned—the list would include some of the most important thinkers and artists of the last few centuries—would not have wasted their time studying a language that made no sense, that its speaker had just made up. Yet we have to admit that this is one of the problems in esoteric studies. That accounts of this inner knowledge often differ, sometimes radically, has led many people to reject it. If these 'secret' meanings of the Bible—or anything else—differ from each other, how can we tell which are valuable and which not? How do we judge one from the other? What gauge do we use to differentiate deep insight from mad raving?

That is a good question. The fact is that the insights and knowledge that come from these pursuits cannot be proven in the way that a mathematical formula or empirical or historical fact can be. Their evidence does not come in that form. It is not public in that way. If it were then practically all the important questions about human existence would have been answered by now. Esoteric knowledge, it seems, falls under what the seventeenth-century French religious thinker and mathematician Blaise Pascal called the *esprit de finesse* and not the *esprit de géométrique*, the spirit of finesse, not geometry.[24]

Dictionaries define finesse as 'great skill', 'style' or 'delicacy', a way of handling a situation with ease. These are correct, but what Pascal means by the 'spirit of finesse' is something more. It's a way of knowing something that can't be spelled out in the same way that we can show that 2+2 = 4. It means a way of knowing something implicitly, a 'felt', 'tacit' knowledge, as the philosopher Michael Polanyi called it.[25] It's a knowledge that often can't be explained explicitly, but only experienced. And in matters of symbolism and interpretation, of hermeneutics and the art of understanding something, multiple insights, sometimes contradictory, can arise from the same source.

I say this merely to point out that in giving some examples of how Swedenborg read Scripture I am not saying that his exegesis is the correct one, and all others wrong—although some dogmatists might think this about his or their own favourite's interpretation. (That way lies fanaticism.) What is important is not that we get our hands on the right interpretation—as fundamentalists claim—but that we are able to widen our understanding of things to include the kind of inner meanings that Swedenborg and other spiritual hermeneuts are offering.

*

Readers interested in a one-to-one checklist of Swedenborg's correspondences can consult George Nicholson's *Dictionary of Correspondences*,[26] a hefty tome that was started in the years after Swedenborg's death and which has been updated ever since; the most recent edition in 2010 runs to some four hundred pages. What I can offer here is an illustration of how Swedenborg's mind worked.

As an example of Swedenborg's inner reading let's take something as commonplace as the sun. The sun, which is the centre of our solar system, provides us with light and warmth. Without it, life would be impossible. We can say that the sun is the source of life and the means of sustaining it. For Swedenborg, the sun plays the same role in the natural world that the Divine does in the spiritual world; it is, in fact, a reflection of the 'spiritual sun', which William Blake claimed to have seen one afternoon on Primrose Hill in North London.[27] But while here the sun illuminates and warms our natural bodies, in the spiritual world these physical functions take on a spiritual character. For Swedenborg, in the spiritual world the sun's light is divine understanding and its warmth divine love. And in the spiritual world these are experienced, as is everything else, as inner states, changes in consciousness.

If 'functions' above sounds too utilitarian, even physiological, we should remember that along with his doctrine of correspondences Swedenborg also developed a doctrine of uses.

This recognizes that everything in existence has some purpose, some use, even in heaven, where, Swedenborg tells us, no angel is idle. There are no free lunches. In its broadest sense this means that creation is no arbitrary collection of galaxies and planets, scattered in the void, but exhibits a meaningful, purposeful order, what used to be called intelligent design.

This idea is not as outdated as we might think. In contemporary terms, we can say that Swedenborg's *Maximus Homo* is a kind of 'anthropic cosmological principle' writ large. The anthropic cosmological principle is a relatively recent way of looking at the universe, which has stirred up not a little controversy. There are different formulations of this principle, but the strongest version of it is the idea that our universe is one in which intelligent life forms like ourselves not only *can* but *must* come into existence.[28] The argument requires recognizing a number of 'cosmic coincidences' that have somehow made it 'just right' for humans like ourselves to appear, such as the size of our sun, our distance from it, the presence of our moon and of 'gas giant' planets like Saturn and Jupiter. There are many other cosmic coincidences that seem to make conditions just right for intelligent life like us, and the reader can find them in *Cosmic Coincidences* by John Gribbin and Martin Rees,[29] as well as in other books dealing with this question.

This in itself is a kind of anti-Copernican shift in our way of seeing our place in the cosmos. Ever since Nicolaus Copernicus we've got used to the idea that we are not at the centre of the universe, and have accepted the shrinking in stature that comes with this knowledge. By now many of us accept that the universe is a meaningless product of a pointless explosion some fifteen billion years ago, and that human life has no particular significance in it. The anthropic cosmological principle tells us that while the earth may not be at the centre of things in terms of space—which, it turns out, may not actually have a centre—the whole affair is nevertheless put on just for us, and the others like us who may be out there. Swedenborg agreed with this but went further. He said that the universe itself was human and that it was created in order to produce humans, who could go on to become angels and so populate heaven, which also has a human form.

*

We've seen that the spiritual sun in that human heaven radiates divine love and wisdom. We understand things by its light and care for them by its warmth. And here on earth we experience a version of this. In our everyday speech we associate light or vision with knowledge and understanding, and warmth with love and tenderness. That is to say that we have some sense of this spiritual sun even on this natural plane. If we understand what someone is telling us we say we 'see what they mean'. If something triggers a sudden beneficial change in our behaviour, we say we 'saw the light'. Someone who grasps complex situations quickly and can 'see' where they will lead we call a 'visionary' who has deep 'insight'. If we want someone to tell us what they know we ask them to 'enlighten' us. We call intelligent youngsters 'bright' and intelligent adults 'brilliant'. The whole movement of the eighteenth century celebrating the rise of reason, rationality and the knowledge they provide, and of which Swedenborg himself was a part, is known as the Enlightenment, just as the time in history following the collapse of the Classical Age, when the learning of the ancients was for the most part lost, is called the Dark Ages. And lest we forget, a seeker of wisdom in the Eastern sense is in search of 'enlightenment'.

The same is true of warmth. We call a loving person 'warm'. If we begin to like someone we say we are 'warming' to them. An email from an old friend 'warms' our heart, and we say of someone who is caring and tender that they have a 'warm heart'. Likewise, someone who strikes us as unfeeling and indifferent is 'cold' or 'heartless'. Mention of the heart reminds us that in Swedenborg's 'useful' anthropomorphic way of seeing things, the physical heart, which represents love, also represents the will. This is because we are moved to act, to will, by our love—our 'true affections' are what drive our decisions. We will what we love and when we really want to accomplish something, we put our 'heart' into it. If we are committed to some action, we 'give it our heart', as well as our soul.

The lungs, on the other hand, are associated—correspond—with our understanding and discernment. In the esoteric reading of the four elements, air is associated with the intellect; fire, or warmth, with the will or creative energy. In a way we can see this as a great 'yes' and 'no' within us, our enthusiastic heart and our discriminating lungs. Things go best when they work together; sadly often they are at odds, with the lungs cooling, if not blowing out, the warm fires of the heart or stoking them to a flaming rage.

The functions that these organs perform in their natural state are also fulfilled in heaven, where whole communities of angels are dedicated to carrying out these tasks, and whose activity constitutes the heavenly equivalent of their earthly counterpart. The angels who correspond to the heart inhabit the celestial heaven and are closest to the Divine, as love is God's greatest expression, sustaining all existence. The angels who correspond to the lungs or divine wisdom inhabit the spiritual heaven, somewhat further away from the source. When we get to the natural world, the divine love and wisdom that sustains existence continues to sustain our life, in the perpetual work of our heart pumping blood and of our lungs drawing air.

*

There is a remarkable economy in Swedenborg's doctrine of correspondences, with the same work being carried out in the same way at all levels of reality, from the air we breathe and the blood in our veins to the divine wisdom and love pervading creation. This reiterative structure, with repetitions of the same design occurring at different levels, is reminiscent in many ways of the physicist David Bohm's notion of an 'implicate order', a hidden unity underlying the apparent multiplicity of the world.[30] It is also reminiscent of the way holograms work, three-dimensional laser images, each part of which contains the whole. And it is also similar to the reiterative pattern of fractals, complex mathematical models associated with chaos theory, that are made of smaller and smaller repetitions of the same basic design, stretching into a microcosmic infinity.

This analogical way of seeing things, with a part containing a whole, seems to have been at work in Swedenborg from early on. Even in his early scientific writing, before he was made privy to the secrets of heaven—the English for *Arcana Caelestia*—Swedenborg seemed to see the activities of the human body in an anthropomorphic way. As Lars Bergquist, Swedenborg's biographer, remarked, Swedenborg was 'characterized throughout his long life by a striking desire and ability to make his feelings concrete and human'.[31] This led to a pictorial or figurative way of seeing things, which is already halfway to recognizing correspondences. If, as Bergquist suggests, Swedenborg's angels give a face to love—as the natural world gives a face to the Divine—he was happy to provide similar analogical accounts of less angelic phenomena. For example, in *The Economy of the Animal Kingdom*, Swedenborg writes of the body's 'pipes, ovens and little bladders' and remarks on how they 'co-operate' with each other. He speaks of a 'grateway of the ribs', and of 'old blood. . .clad in black garments hurried away to the tombs of the liver'. There are 'hungry veins' that 'eagerly snatch' at gastric juices, and he describes the activity of nerves as like a 'married pair, the intercostals doing the husband's office and the par vagum the wife's'.[32]

This penchant for picturing his thoughts and insights was part and parcel of how Swedenborg's mind worked. We can see it at the heart of his insight that we 'create our own reality', in the sense that the world we inhabit is an 'out-picturing' of the thoughts we entertain. Heaven and hell, we know, are inside us and we transform our outside world into one or the other by our 'true affections'. When Swedenborg left earth and entered the spiritual worlds, it's not surprising that his tendency to communicate what he learned in images and analogies would continue, and that he would provide for his many readers a kind of 'Rough Guide' to higher realms, full of memorable descriptions.

Yet if Swedenborg's human way of seeing things seems to carry analogies too far, we should consider this. If, as he says, the universe is like us, then that also means that we are like it. This is the basic idea behind the most famous doctrine of correspondences in the West, even more well known than Swedenborg's, the 'as above, so below' of Hermes Trismegistus, father of astrology, magic, alchemy and the Hermetic tradition. The saying comes from the most famous alchemical text, Hermes' fabled *Emerald Tablet*, a work first believed to have been written in the dim dawn of time, but which scholarship dates to the eighth century. 'As above, so below' is the formula of the microcosm and the macrocosm, the little and big cosmos, the human being and the universe, the Hermetic version of Swedenborg's *Maximus Homo*. For it, as for Swedenborg, as things are in the heavens, so too are they on earth. If Swedenborg was not alone in developing a way of grasping the inner meaning of Scripture, he was also not alone in trying to understand the inner harmony between man and the world in which he finds himself.

*

As with Swedenborg, in the Hermetic tradition,

man, the human being, is at the centre of things. We contain within ourselves the entire range of reality, from the natural world and the cosmos, to the higher spheres. As the Hermetic writings tell us, man is a 'divine being' and 'is not to be counted amongst the other creatures on earth'.[33] This is not to encourage delusions of grandeur, or give us carte blanche to lord it over the rest of creation, but to recognize our unique place and responsibility in the scheme of things, and to inspire us to fulfil it. For Hermes, human beings are even above the gods, because while they and the angels are fixed in their places in the great cosmic plan, we, the thrice-great sage tells us, are free to rise to the heights or plunge to the depths, partaking of all the universe has to offer, a point the Renaissance Hermeticist Pico della Mirandola made in his famous *Oration on the Dignity of Man*.[34] As with Swedenborg's 'true affections', for the Hermetic tradition, it is our free choices that decide whether we explore the peaks of human reality, or enjoy the lowlands of the soul.

Because he contains the entire world within himself, in the Hermetic tradition man is privy to the links running through all creation, what the Neoplatonic philosophers called 'the sympathy of all things', the *anima mundi* or 'soul of the world', the equivalent of Swedenborg's correspondences. This is perhaps the single most important belief in the esoteric tradition. It certainly receives pride of place in the 'fundamental elements of esotericism' of the esoteric scholar Antoine Faivre, who held the chair in the History of Esoteric and Mystical Currents in Modern Europe at the Sorbonne in Paris. In this tradition, Faivre writes, 'Symbolic and real correspondences. . . are said to exist among all parts of the universe, both seen and unseen', what Faivre calls a 'universal interdependence'. As with Swedenborg, these correspondences are 'more or less veiled at first sight' but are 'intended to be read and deciphered'. As Faivre tells us, the 'entire universe is a huge theatre of mirrors, an ensemble of hieroglyphics to be decoded'.[35]

The essence of the Hermetic science is to learn the clues that will allow one to break the code so that one can read, as the seventeenth-century Hermetic philosopher Jacob Boehme did, the 'signature of all things'.[36] This knowledge came to Boehme, a Bohemian cobbler, in a flash, when a glint of sunlight on a pewter dish sent him into a mystical state, and he was 'introduced into the innermost ground or centre of the recondite or hidden nature'.[37] Boehme said he learned more in the few minutes in which this state lasted than he would have had he spent years at university. He went on to convey his insight in a series of books, written in a darkly evocative language, that influenced important thinkers such as the philosopher Hegel and the poets Blake and Coleridge, among many others.

One suspects Boehme may have seen into the heart of things as Swedenborg would later; certainly the speed of learning both experienced seems similar. Swedenborg said of his conversations with angels that they 'can express within a minute what we cannot in half an hour' and that they 'can express in one word what we cannot with a thousand'.[38] Elsewhere I have written about the correspondences between the speed and density of Swedenborg's angelic conversations, and the similar acceleration of understanding that was required of Hermes Trismegistus, when he received the revelation at the heart of the Hermetic tradition from the divine mind, *Nous*.[39] As I point out, other voyagers into the upper reaches of consciousness, such as the philosopher and psychologist William James, left accounts that echo Swedenborg's and Hermes', suggesting that the experience is somehow universal.

Faivre points out that there are two levels of correspondence, what we might call the 'natural' and the 'scriptural', both of which would have been familiar to Swedenborg. For Faivre, the 'natural' correspondences, which include the 'seen and unseen', are those that run between the seven planets and seven metals of alchemy, the constellations dominant at one's birth and one's fate, and the 'like cures like' analogical medicine of alchemist healers like the sixteenth-century Swiss Paracelsus, father of modern pharmacology.[40] These correspondences run between the cosmos and the human body and echo what Swedenborg has to tell us about the *Maximus Homo*.

They also relate to Adam Kadmon, the Universal Man of cabbala, another esoteric teaching that has correspondence at its heart, with its mystical Tree of Life growing throughout the universe, the higher worlds—which parallel in many ways Swedenborg's account—and ourselves. It is the connectedness of all things that allows for magic to work, with the part standing in for the whole, making it susceptible to 'action at a distance', and the symbol or sigil of the required power—angelic or demonic—serving as a conductor of its force.

This correspondence is in fact at the heart of our experiencing the world at all. As Plotinus wrote 'never did eye see the sun unless it had first become sun-like'.[41] We would not perceive a world if there was not a world within us, and the world we do perceive corresponds to that inner one.

The other correspondence, the 'scriptural', is the one Swedenborg started out seeking to grasp. This is the concordance between the cosmos and holy or revealed texts, such as the Bible. It is here that the kind of 'spiritual hermeneutics' explored by Henry Corbin comes into play. This is the art of divining the hidden meaning, the depth (*batin* or 'esoteric' in Arabic) both announced and obscured by the surface (*zahir* or 'exoteric') meaning of a text, a kind of archaeology of understanding that is also at the heart of cabbala. This discipline, which Corbin refers to as *ta'wil*, attempts to 'look through' texts—and the phenomena of the world—making them translucent, so that the surface and the depth, the outer and inner, are perceived simultaneously. If the surface, that of a text or a thing, simultaneously points to and hides a depth, then *ta'wil* is a way of uniting the two.

*

It should come as no surprise that the twelfth-century Persian Gnostic philosopher Suhrawardi, whose study led Corbin to the pursuit of *ta'wil*, wrote of his own journeys into the higher worlds in ways similar to Swedenborg. Like Swedenborg, Suhrawardi's accounts of the spiritual worlds are full-bodied visionary tales, in which different states of consciousness are symbolized by characters and settings in a narrative, a story; like Swedenborg, Suhrawardi is a concrete, not abstract thinker. As Corbin writes, Suhrawardi translated 'inner spiritual states' into 'vision events' that depicted a setting and story embodying these simultaneously deeper and higher levels of consciousness.

Corbin writes that on his inner journeys, Suhrawardi entered a kind of waking dream, and he remarks that the best time for doing this is in the liminal phase between sleeping and waking known as the hypnagogic state. Swedenborg is known to have mastered a way of remaining in this state for extended periods, and it was in them that he, like Suhrawardi, journeyed to inner worlds. And just as Swedenborg found this inner space occupied by its own inhabitants, so too, Corbin tells us, did Suhrawardi. It was to distinguish this inner but objective space—an interior realm possessed of its own geography, history, even occupants—from what we usually mean by the 'subjective', that Corbin coined the term 'imaginal'.

This was something different from the merely imaginary, the world of 'make believe'. For Corbin, the kind of journeys that Suhrawardi, Swedenborg and other inner voyagers make, take place in what he calls the *Mundus Imaginalis*, or Imaginal World.[42] This is the world of symbols, images and visionary states, set between the physical world available to our senses and the austere world of pure ideas, grasped solely by the intellect. It is a world of 'concrete imagination', of visions that are embodied but not physical, inner but not subjective, and which reveal a territory of interior landscapes and inhabitants that possess an objective, independent reality of their own.

Other inner travellers have made similar reports. The psychologist Carl Jung, another reader of Swedenborg, claimed that during his 'descent into the unconscious', from which he brought back the fundamental ideas of the 'collective unconscious', he had encountered beings who inhabited his inner world, but who had a life of their own, independent of him.[43] In his follow up to *The Doors of Perception*, *Heaven and Hell*, a title taken from Swedenborg as the earlier book's was taken from Blake's *The Marriage of Heaven and Hell*, Aldous Huxley spoke of his experiences of altered consciousness. He said that 'Like the earth of a hundred years ago, our mind still has its darkest Africa, its unmapped Borneos and Amazonian basins'. (Huxley was writing more than half a century ago.) He spoke of the 'far continents' of the mind, its 'antipodes', what he called 'Mind-at-

Large,' and of their 'improbable' inhabitants, whose 'complete autonomy' and 'self-sufficiency', were, however unlikely, nevertheless 'facts of observation'.[44]

Huxley's remark about the flora and fauna of the inner worlds being 'facts of observation' reminds us that Corbin stressed that the Imaginal World is 'a very precise order of reality which corresponds to a precise mode of perception'.[45] It was not a world in which fantasy, or imagination in the negative sense, ran riot, but was made up of what another inner voyager and reader of Swedenborg, the poet Samuel Taylor Coleridge, called 'facts of mind'.[46] The Imaginal World was not random, arbitrary or capricious, but followed its own laws and necessities. And in order to navigate through it, inner voyagers needed to know these laws, just as a good boatman must know the character of the river on which he travels. Corbin warned of the need of a tradition, which he characterized as a 'cosmology. . .with a plurality of universes arranged in an ascending order', the ladder of worlds we have looked at in Swedenborg. Without such a tradition to guide the inner voyager, there was a danger, Corbin feared, that the imagination will go astray, and its 'recurrent conjunctions with our will-to-power' become a 'never-ending source of horror'.[47]

When Corbin wrote these words, in the late 1970s, the traditional view of reality he referred to had long been absent from the modern mind, and the images and symbols produced by modern culture pointed more towards a chaos of competing subjectivities, often very violent ones, than any shared ground of vision. Corbin recognized, as did Owen Barfield, that there is a 'responsibility of the imagination',[48] and that without accepting and embracing this, we can easily find ourselves adrift in a world of fantasy, the very realm of 'make believe' that is the opposite of the Imaginal World. And as Barfield and Corbin both recognized, everything there is not all sweetness and light, something that the intervening years since they voiced their concerns seem to have only helped to make even more obvious.

*

At the beginning of this essay I remarked that the most successful adaptation of Swedenborg's doctrine of correspondences was that which led to the Symbolist movement of the nineteenth century. The man responsible for this was Charles Baudelaire. Let's end this look at Swedenborg's correspondences with a glance at what Baudelaire did with them, and with this question: what part did Baudelaire's interpretation of Swedenborg's doctrine play in our arriving at the situation that worried Barfield and Corbin?

It's unclear how much of Swedenborg Baudelaire actually read. While he may have read a French translation of *Heaven and Hell*, it seems that much of his knowledge of Swedenborg's ideas came from the work of another French writer, Honoré de Balzac (1799-1850). Balzac wrote of Swedenborg's philosophy in two books, *Louis Lambert* and his mystical novel *Seraphita*, whose gender-swapping eponymous hero/heroine, is a symbol of the original, unfallen, androgynous character of the soul. What seems to have happened is that Baudelaire took Swedenborg's doctrine of correspondences and combined it with ideas coming from two writers who had a great influence on him, both of whom, as we might have guessed, were also interested in Swedenborg.

From the German writer of weird tales E T A Hoffmann, most remembered today by lovers of Offenbach and Tchaikovsky, Baudelaire took the notion of synaesthesia, the strange phenomenon of one sense doing the work of—or corresponding to—another. With synaesthesia one can hear colours and see sounds. Hoffmann was particularly prone to this, and spoke of being attuned to 'an analogy and close union between colours, sounds, and scents'. The scent of brown and red marigolds, for example, produced in him 'the far off sound of an oboe'. [49] One of Hoffmann's characters, the Kapellmeister Johannes Kreisler—Hoffmann was also a brilliant music critic—wears a coat that is in C sharp minor with a collar in E major. 'It is no empty metaphor', Hoffmann wrote, 'when a musician says that colour, fragrance, light appear to him as sounds'.[50] Fundamentally Hoffmann believed that all the phenomena of the senses originate in the same source—some primal unified sense—and that they were destined to reunite in a 'wonderful concert', just as all the colours of the rainbow come together in white light.[51]

This notion of the unity of the senses, and by extension, that of the arts, would find its most powerful expression in the operas of Richard Wagner, who aimed at creating a *Gesamtkunstwerk*, a 'total art work' that would bring music, drama, colour and movement together into a single performance. The Russian composer and Theosophist Alexander Scriabin tried to go one better than Wagner with an enormous work he envisioned but was unable to complete. His *Mysterium*, left unfinished at the time of his death, required a full orchestra and choir, but also demanded incense, dancers and a colour wheel (an early light show that would project colours on a screen corresponding to the music). Scriabin planned for this gargantuan work to be performed in a temple in the foothills of the Himalayas, the culmination of a week-long festival, reminiscent of the ancient Greek Mysteries. Other artists, like the painter Wassily Kandinsky, the novelist Vladimir Nabokov and the composer Olivier Messiaen, were also strong synaesthetes. Arthur Rimbaud, mentioned earlier, created a kind of synaesthetic alphabet in his poem 'Vowels', which links each vowel with a colour and paints A black, E white, I red, U green, and O blue.

While Hoffmann was a serious student of Swedenborg's ideas, as well as those of his contemporary, the scientist and healer Franz Anton Mesmer, the other writer Baudelaire borrowed from was less respectful. Edgar

Allan Poe seems not to have read much Swedenborg, but he became aware of Mesmer's ideas about 'magnetic trance'—which, at the time, were often blended with notions of Swedenborg's visionary states—from a book *Facts in Mesmerism* by Revd Chauncey Hare Townshend.[52] His ignorance of Swedenborg, however, did not prevent Poe from writing a story, 'Mesmeric Revelation', that so impressed a Swedenborgian group with its insights, that they wrote to Poe, praising him for his accurate account of the higher worlds. (Typically Poe wrote back, saying he had made it up.)[53] Oddly enough, 'Mesmeric Revelation' was the first of Poe's stories that Baudelaire translated into French. For much of his career, Baudelaire was more well known for his Poe translations than for his own poetry.

What Baudelaire took from Poe—with whom he seemed to be obsessed—was the idea of the poet as a kind of seer, a mystic, an individual sensitive to nuances and subtleties of reality to which the coarser-minded philistines were simply blind. In the rough and tumble America of the early nineteenth century, this character trait made Poe stick out like a sore thumb, but it made him attractive to the French. Poe, too, like Hoffmann, was familiar with synaesthesia; in his *Marginalia* he writes 'The orange ray of the spectrum and the buzz of the gnat . . . affect me with nearly similar sensations'.[54] Baudelaire was also not immune, and in his *Salon of 1846*, he complained of a tavern's façade that its red and green was for him a 'source of exquisite pain'.[55]

With help from Hoffmann and Poe, Baudelaire took Swedenborg's correspondences and changed their direction. From pointing vertically—at the higher worlds—he now turned them horizontally. The correspondences now were not between the natural world and the higher worlds above, but between the different experiences of the senses. This was something Baudelaire spelled out in his poem 'Correspondences', which marks the start of the Symbolist movement. In it he tells us that 'Nature' is a 'temple' whose 'living pillars' emit 'confused words', and as we walk through its 'forests of symbols' it observes us with 'familiar glances'. There, in a 'dark and profound unity', 'perfumes, colours, and sounds respond'. Some perfumes are 'sweet like oboes' and others suggest the 'expanse of infinite things'. But they all conspire to produce in the poet 'ecstasies of the mind and senses'.[56]

So, from pointing to a higher, non-sensory world, the correspondences were now the medium of sensual delight. Yet these ecstasies are not available to everyone. Only the poet as seer is able to interpret these strange symbols, which tell him that the everyday world is somehow other than what it seems. To the average bourgeois they are meaningless. The 'ensemble of hieroglyphics' waiting 'to be decoded'[57] of which Antoine Faivre tells us, could now be translated solely through the Rosetta Stone of the poet's sensitivity. As the critic Anna

Balakian writes, 'with his superior network of senses and perception', the poet was now 'bent on deciphering, rather than conveying or communicating, the enigmas of life'.[58]

It's not surprising that a view of the world that paints it as less solid and obdurate than it seems came to prominence during a time when the materialist view, which remains in place today, was quickly establishing its dominance. When Baudelaire's 'Correspondences' appeared, the Industrial Revolution had only recently triumphed. As the everyday world became more and more a question of 'matter'—confirming the 'reign of quantity'[59] of the Traditionalist philosopher René Guénon—it seems that in compensation, artists and poets began to turn it into one of mist and shadows, fleeting, flickering glimpses, suggesting something else, just out of reach, hovering behind the scenes, that could not be quantified or measured or put to profit.

As we've seen, Baudelaire's turning Swedenborg's correspondences on their side was a remarkably fertile idea. But at its heart it had a fatal flaw. It lacked the kind of objectivity that Baudelaire, who possessed the 'precise mode of perception'[60] necessary for *ta'wil*, demanded of his art and which Swedenborg claimed from the start. In the *Salon of 1846* Baudelaire had asked if a 'well authenticated scale of colours and their corresponding feelings' had been drawn up by an 'analogist', that could account for their effect on sensitive natures, such as his own.[61] Baudelaire believed that the synaesthetic effect of Wagner's music on himself and others was the same, but this finding was not corroborated. In fact, if one studies the correspondences experienced by different synaesthetes, one discovers that there is rarely any unanimity among them. Hoffmann may have heard the sound of an oboe when sniffing marigolds, but not everyone did, not even other synaesthetes. The one-to-one correspondences that Swedenborg had mapped between the natural and higher worlds, had quickly given way to a wider horizontal application which was steadily dissolving the inner meaning of phenomena into a more and more vague and seductively suggestive fog of subjective symbolism, rising out of the artist's and poet's own personal vocabulary.

While early Romantics, like Goethe and Blake, knew and embraced the traditional 'cosmology' that Henry Corbin saw was needed, and used their symbolic language responsibly, their epigones were less securely anchored. As Czesław Miłosz wrote, 'by shifting the emphasis', the Symbolists 'obtained the opposite' of Swedenborg's original idea. 'Correspondences are not symbols to be arbitrarily chosen by a poet or novelist', Miłosz points out. Instead they are linked by a necessity, 'preordained by God and determined by the very structure of nature and the human imagination'. They were not 'destined to become a basis for legitimizing uncontrolled subjectivity or for establishing a democratic equality of subjective symbols and metaphors'.[62]

But that, unfortunately or otherwise, is exactly what happened. And now, more than a century after the Symbolist heyday, even the vague evocation of 'another' world that its masters conveyed with great power and magic is valued little more than as decoration for a period piece. In our post-everything times, the idea that things around us are connected to some higher realm gets little attention and the material explanations of life and reality that the Symbolists wanted to resist remain more firmly in place than ever. And the arts themselves, that once resisted these explanations, have become, according to one critic, 'the expression of the very incoherence and ignorance from which they normally provide release'.[63]

If Swedenborg's correspondences were designed to secure a necessary bond between the natural and spiritual worlds, thereby giving the natural world meaning, in the same way that a word's meaning makes it something more than an arbitrary collection of letters—as suggested at the start of this essay—then we have to accept that, for the time being at least, that connection has been broken. Or, if not broken, at least become obscure, so that today we find ourselves not safely harboured in the macrocosm, but somewhat adrift in the cosmos. But what is lost can be found and what is forgotten can be remembered. And Swedenborg's writings remain as very good reminders of what we are looking for.

Endnotes

1 Emanuel Swedenborg, *Arcana Coelestia*, published in Latin, 1749-56.
2 Emanuel Swedenborg, *Heaven and Hell*, tr. K C Ryder (London: Swedenborg Society, 2010), §89, p. 61.
3 See Johann Wolfgang von Goethe, *Faust I & II*, tr. Stuart Atkins (Princeton: Princeton University Press, 1994), Part II, Act V, p. 305.
4 Czesław Miłosz, 'Introduction', in O V de L Milosz, *The Noble Traveller: The Life and Writings of O. V. de L. Milosz*, ed. Christopher Bamford (West Stockbridge, MA: Lindisfarne Press, 1985), p. 33.
5 Henry Corbin, *Swedenborg and Esoteric Islam*, tr. Leonard Fox (West Chester, PA: Swedenborg Foundation, 1995), p. 35.
6 Swedenborg, *Heaven and Hell*, §89, p. 61.
7 Ibid., §87, p. 60.

8 Gertrude Stein, *Geography and Plays* (Madison, WI: University of Wisconsin Press, 2012), p. 187.
9 Emanuel Swedenborg, *Conjugial Love*, first published in Latin in 1768.
10 William Blake, *Europe: A Prophecy* (1794), plate 5, l. 7, in *Complete Writings*, ed. Geoffrey Keynes (Oxford: OUP, 1988), p. 240.
11 Sir Oliver Lodge, *Raymond or Life and Death* (New York: George H Doran Company, 1916), pp. 197-8.
12 Charles Drayton Thomas, *Life Beyond Death With Evidence* (London: W Collins Sons & Company, 1928), pp. 128, 131, 135.
13 Friedrich Nietzche, *Human, All Too Human: A Book for Free Spirits*, first published in German in three volumes between 1878-80.
14 John Keble, 'New Every Morning is the Love' (1822).
15 Goethe, *Faust I & II*, Part I, p. 16.
16 Rudolf Otto, *The Idea of the Holy*, tr. John W Harvey (London: Oxford University Press, 1923), p. 23.
17 Gary Lachman, *Into the Interior: Discovering Swedenborg* (London: Swedenborg Society, 2009), pp. 122-3.
18 See Owen Barfield, *Owen Barfield and the Origin of Language* (Spring Valley, NY: St George Publications, 1979).

19 See Clement of Alexandria, *The Stromata, or Miscellanies* (London: Aeterna Press, 2016), esp. book VI, ch. XIV, 'Degrees of Glory in Heaven', pp. 349-52.
20 Albert C Geljon and David T Runia, 'Preface', in Philo of Alexandria, *On Cultivation*, tr. and ed. Albert C Geljon and David T Runia (Leiden: Brill, 2012), p. xvii.
21 Maurice Nicoll, *The New Man: An Interpretation of Some Parables and Miracles of Christ* (London: Stuart and Richards, 1950) and *The Mark* (London: Vincent Stuart, 1954).
22 Maurice Nicoll, *Psychological Commentaries On the Teachings of G. I. Gurdjieff and P. D. Ouspensky*, 5 vols. (London: Vincent Stuart, 1952) and *Living Time and the Integration of the Life* (London: Vincent Stuart, 1952).
23 Porphyry, *On the Cave of Nymphs in the Thirteenth Book of the Odyssey*, tr. Thomas Taylor (London: John M Watkins, 1917).
24 Blaise Pascal, *Pensées*, ed. Philippe Selliers (Paris: Le Livre de Poche, 2000), p. 670.
25 Michael Polanyi, *The Tacit Dimension* (New York: Anchor Books, 1967).
26 George Nicholson, *A New and Comprehensive Dictionary of Correspondences, Representatives,*

and Significatives, contained in the Word of the Lord (London: J Bonsor, 1800); repr. as *Dictionary of Correspondences: The Key to Biblical Interpretation* (West Chester, PA: Swedenborg Foundation, 2010).

27 Swedenborg, *Heaven and Hell*, §§116-25, pp. 79-85 and *Angelic Wisdom concerning the Divine Love and Wisdom*, tr. Clifford and Doris Harley (London: Swedenborg Society, 1987), §93, pp. 36-7. Henry Crabb Robinson, diary entry for 10 December 1825, in *Diary, Reminiscences, and Correspondence of Henry Crabb Robinson*, ed. Thomas Sadler, 2 vols. (London and New York: Macmillan and Co., 1872)), vol. II, p. 9.

28 John D Barrow and Frank J Tipler, *The Anthropic Cosmological Principle* (Oxford: Clarendon, 1985).

29 John Gribbin and Martin Rees, *Cosmic Coincidences: Dark Matter, Mankind, and Anthropic Cosmology* (New York: Bantam New Age, 1989).

30 David Bohm, *Wholeness and the Implicate Order* (London: Routledge, 1980).

31 Lars Bergquist, *Swedenborg's Secret: A Biography*, tr. Norman Ryder (London: Swedenborg Society, 2005), p. 167.

32 Emanuel Swedenborg, *The Economy of the Animal*

Kingdom, tr. Augustus Clissold, 2 vols. (London: W Newbery, 1845-6), vol. I, p. 175, vol. II, p. 83, vol. I, pp. 168, 166, 474.

33 Clement Salaman, *Asclepius: The Perfect Discourse of Hermes Trismegistus* (London: Duckworth, 2007), p. 63.

34 Pico della Mirandola, *Oration on the Dignity of Man*, tr. A Robert Gaponigri (Washington, D.C.: Gateway Editions, 1996). Pico della Mirandola's *Oration on the Dignity of Man* was composed in Latin in 1486 and first printed posthumously in 1496.

35 Antoine Faivre, *Access to Western Esotericism* (Albany: State University of New York Press, 1994), p. 10.

36 Jacob Boehme wrote *De Signatura Rerum* in High Dutch in 1621 and it was published posthumously in 1635. It was first published in English as *Signatura Rerum: or the Signature of all Things*, tr. John Ellistone (London: John Macock, 1651).

37 Francis Okely, *Memoirs of the Life, Death, Burial, and Wonderful Writings, of Jacob Behmen* (Northampton: Theo. Dicey, 1780), pp. 7-8.

38 Swedenborg, *Heaven and Hell*, §240, p. 154.

39 See Gary Lachman, *The Quest for Hermes Trismegistus: From Ancient Egypt to the Modern World* (Edinburgh: Floris Books, 2011).

40 Faivre, *Access to Western Esotericism*, pp. 10-11.
41 Plotinus, *The Enneads*, tr. Stephen Mackenna (Burdett, NY: Larson Publications,1992), p. 72.
42 See Henry Corbin, 'Mundus Imaginalis, or the Imaginary and the Imaginal', in *Swedenborg and Esoteric Islam*, pp. 1-33.
43 See Carl Gustav Jung, *Analytical Psychology: Notes of the Seminar Given in 1925*, ed. William McGuire (Princeton, NJ: Princeton University Press, 1991).
44 Aldous Huxley, *Heaven and Hell* (New York: Harper, 1956), pp. 1-4, 63 (Mind-at-Large).
45 Corbin, 'Mundus Imaginalis', p. 1.
46 S T Coleridge, letter to John Thelwall, 19 November 1796, in *Letters of Samuel Taylor Coleridge*, ed. Ernest Hartley Coleridge, 2 vols. (Boston and New York: Houghton, Mifflin and Company, 1895), vol. I, p. 181.
47 Corbin, 'Mundus Imaginalis', p. 19.
48 See Owen Barfield, *A Barfield Reader*, ed. G B Tennyson (Hanover and London: Wesleyan University Press, 1999), p. 157.
49 E T A Hoffmann, *Kreisleriana*, quoted in Charles Baudelaire, *The Salon of 1846*, in *Selected Writings on Art and Artists*, tr. P E Charvet (Cambridge: Cambridge University Press, 1981), p. 58.
50 E T A Hoffmann, *E. T. A. Hoffmann's Musical*

Writings: Kreisleriana; The Poet and the Composer; Music Criticism (Cambridge: Cambridge University Press, 2003), p. 164.

51 Hoffmann, *Kreisleriana*, quoted in Baudelaire, *The Salon of 1846*, p. 58.

52 Chauncey Hare Townshend, *Facts in Mesmerism, with Reasons for a Dispassionate Enquiry into it* (London: Longman, Orme, Brown, Green, & Longmans, 1840).

53 Edgar Allan Poe, 'Mesmeric Revelation', in *Columbian Magazine*, vol. 2, no. 1, August 1844, pp. 67-70; and 'Marginal Notes.—No. 1', in *Godey's Lady's Book*, vol. XXXI, August 1845, p. 50.

54 Edgar Allan Poe, 'Marginalia [part I]', in *United States Magazine and Democratic Review*, vol. XV, no. LXXVII, November 1844, p. 490.

55 Baudelaire, *Selected Writing on Art and Artists*, p. 58.

56 Charles Baudelaire, 'Correspondences', in *The Flowers of Evil & Paris Spleen: Selected Poems*, tr. Wallace Fowlie (Mineola, NY: Dover Publications, 2010), p. 10.

57 Faivre, *Access to Western Esotericism*, p. 10.

58 Anna Balakian, *The Symbolist Movement: A Critical Appraisal* (New York: Random House, 1967), p. 47.

59 René Guénon, *The Reign of Quantity and the*

Signs of the Times, tr. Lord Northbourne (Hillsdale, NY: Sophia Perennis, 2001).

60 Corbin, 'Mundus Imaginalis', p. 1.

61 Baudelaire, *Selected Writing on Art and Artists*, p. 58.

62 Czesław Miłosz, *Emperor of the Earth: Modes of Eccentric Vision* (Berkeley: University of California Press, 1981), p. 128.

63 Kathleen Raine, *Defending Ancient Springs* (Oxford: Oxford University Press, 1967), p. 165.

Swedenborg: select works

1709	*Selected Sentences*
1714	*Ludus Heliconius*
1715	*Festivus Applausus*
	Camena Borea
1716-18	*Daedalus Hyperboreus*
1721	*A New Method of finding the Longitude*
1722	*Miscellaneous Observations,* pts 1, 2, 3 & 4
1734	*The Infinite The Final Cause of Creation/The Mechanism of the Operation of the Soul and Body*
1734	*Opera Philosophica et Mineralia*, 3 vols.
1740-1	*The Economy of the Animal Kingdom*, pts 1 & 2
1744-5	*The Animal Kingdom*, pts 1, 2 & 3
1745	*The Worship and Love of God*, pts 1 & 2
1749-56	*Arcana Caelestia*, 8 vols.
1758	*The Worlds in Space*
	Heaven and Hell
	The Last Judgment
	The New Jerusalem and Its Heavenly Doctrine

	The White Horse
1763	*The New Jerusalem concerning The Lord*
	The New Jerusalem concerning Sacred Scripture
	The New Jerusalem concerning Life
	The New Jerusalem concerning Faith
	Continuation on the Last Judgment
	Divine Love and Wisdom
1764	*Divine Providence*
1766	*The Apocalypse Revealed*
1768	*Conjugial Love*
1769	*Brief Exposition of the Doctrines of the New Church*
	The Interaction of the Soul & Body
1771	*The True Christian Religion*

— OTHER TITLES —

Introducing Swedenborg

Peter Ackroyd

'Ackroyd is a medium through which
the obscured voices of the past are channeled.'
—*Newsday*

Skilfully written and carefully researched, award-winning biographer Peter Ackroyd offers an accessible account of one of the world's great polymaths and visionaries. The first in a series of new pocket books, *Introducing Swedenborg* is the perfect introduction to this seminal but often misunderstood giant of the eighteenth century.

PETER ACKROYD is a broadcaster, essayist and one of the UK's foremost biographers and novelists. Among his many awards and honours is the Whitbread Biography Award (1984). He was elected a fellow of the Royal Society of Literature in 1984 and was awarded a CBE in 2003.

— OTHER TITLES —

On the Conjugial Angel

A S Byatt

'. . . one of Britain's foremost grandes dames
of the writing world'
—*The Sunday Telegraph*

Drawn from the transcript of a talk given at Swedenborg House in 2010, *On the Conjugial Angel* explores Swedenborg's influence on literature, the lives of the Tennysons, the conflict between religion and science and offers an intimate insight into A S Byatt's writing methods. It is the sixth volume in the Swedenborg Archive Series.

A S BYATT has written numerous works of fiction including *Possession: A Romance* (1990), for which she won the Booker Prize; *Angels and Insects* (1992) and *The Children's Book* (2009). She was made a Fellow of University College London in 2004 and a Fellow of the British Academy in 2017.

Blake's London: the Topographic Sublime

Iain Sinclair

'A modern-day William Blake'
—Jacques Peretti, BBC *The Culture Show*

What was William Blake's relation with London? And how did this relation shape his poetic visions? In this small and specially designed volume, Iain Sinclair takes the reader on a discursive journey through Blake's London showing how, in Blake's vast and rich poetry, language and imagination conjoin to delineate a profound engagement with place.

IAIN SINCLAIR is a renowned essayist and writer of fiction whose novels include *Downriver* (winner of the James Tait Black Prize and the Encore Prize), *London Orbital* and *Lights Out for the Territory*.

www.swedenborg.org/books